Embrace your MOMENT

DR. FREDRICK J. HARRIS

Published by:
EMPOWER ME BOOKS, INC.
A Subsidiary of Empower Me Enterprises, Inc.
P.O. Box 16153 Durham, North Carolina 27704
www.EmpowerMeBooks.com

Scriptures taken from the Holy Bible, New Living Translation, Copyright © 1996, 2004. Used by permission of Tyndale House Publishers, Inc., Wheaton, Illinois 60189
All rights reserved.
ISBN: 978-1732773110

Printed in The United States of America

PREFACE

I would like to thank everyone who is reading this book to understand that it's time to Embrace Your Moment. I took the liberty, through the guidance of the Holy Spirit, my own personal observations and experiences, and through literature research, to utilize the Word of God for scriptural references.

As well as encompassing the usage of the Merriam-Webster dictionary and FreeDictionary. com, I was able to capture and highlight much of the revelation that is shared in this body of work.

Throughout our time, from generation to generation, evidence has been shown to us what it means to "embrace". The word itself has several meanings; therefore, when you hear this word, you must interpret the essence based upon the situation at hand.

We live in a society that is very progressive and change happens daily. However, as you embrace each moment, there is an opportunity to learn, grow, receive, and process your journey as you move forward to achieve success in your life and to become a positive example in your surroundings.

There is a legacy on the inside of you and it must come forth with inspiration, insight and empowerment. Life has multiple translations to understand, and we all need to be able to improve our communications. When thinking about the digital and technology age of our culture, and how far innovations have brought us over a span of time, we must make an impact or a mark that cannot be erased. You have a dream! You have a plan! Then go for it.

This book offers a unique perspective about what it means to embrace your moment. With over 26 years of military experience, and 19 years of service to the Lord and counting, I have embraced the next assignment to encourage a generation to embrace their moment.

Serving in the marketplace as a middle school educator at a private Christian academy, I have been given an awesome opportunity to infuse tomorrow's leaders to launch out into the deep to discover who they are and what journey awaits them.

Through the writings in this book, you will experience hope, encouragement, impartation and even some humor. There is knowledge to share by all, and I am grateful to be given this space of time to be an oracle of truth for the glory of God.

Embrace your journey! Set a course for yourself to learn everything possible that is going to put you in position for increase and prosperity. If you must reposition yourself periodically, that is fine too. The goal is to never lose your focus or ambition where you are headed.

There are people, places and opportunities that are waiting for you to arrive at your destination. Many people never truly get to that place of blessings because of fear, rejection, doubt and a lack of understanding. I encourage you today to embrace your moment.

Inside this book, there are principles and wisdom nuggets that can unlock destiny and revelation to redirect, or point, to certain keys that will give you the added nudge that's necessary for the next moment.

Finally, my prayer is that God will enlarge your territory and bless you in a phenomenal way so that you can't contain it. Do you want to see something happen? Do you desire to leave a legacy that can't be erased?

What Are You Waiting For? GO FOR IT...

INTRODUCTION

Building A Legacy That Can't Be Erased shall cause you to EMBRACE YOUR MOMENT! -Ecclesiastes 3:10-14 (NIV)

I have seen the burden God has laid on humanity. He has made everything beautiful in its time. He has also set eternity in the human heart, yet no one can fathom what God has done from beginning to end. I know that there is nothing better for people than to be happy and to do good while they live. That each of them may eat and drink and find satisfaction in all of their toil - this is the gift of God. I know that everything God does will endure forever; nothing can be added to it and nothing taken from it. God does it so that people will fear Him.

Embrace:

1. Hold (someone) closely in one's arms, especially as a sign of affection.
2. Accept or support (a belief, theory, or change) willingly and enthusiastically.
3. Include or contain (something) as a constituent part.

Embrace implies a gathering of separate items within a whole. This also means to have inclusion by virtue of the process for which one is faced with, in order to reach a desired outcome. In life, there are going to be challenges and adversities that will arise, and you must encounter these situations as opportunities for wisdom, insight, and instructions. The Word of God is your compass and will help you to have a starting point.

Once you have embraced your direction, it's always a great structure to have individuals who will serve as mentors, advisors, and teachers. Look over your plans and do regular assessments to ensure you are in focus of what you can see and experience.

CHAPTER 1

MISSED OPPORTUNITIES

Everyone has missed opportunities to do something good, to help somebody, or even the chance at a promotion of some sort. However, discouragement of some kind has its room to settle into your psyche; you do not want to think you're mediocre because of this missed opportunity. Through observation, I have learned to rise to the occasion because of an epic fail.

I often mention to people in various conversations that "you can rise from the ashes". R.I.S.E. means Restoration and Insight for Seasons of Empowerment. You will be raised to a higher standard for kingdom advancement as you continue to keep thanksgiving in your mouth for the Lord. Your enemies shall see you triumph with victory in your hands. Psalm 41:1-3 (NLT) states "Oh, the joys of those who are kind to the poor! The Lord rescues them when they are in trouble. The Lord protects them and keeps them alive. He gives them prosperity in the land and rescues them from their enemies. The Lord nurses them when they are sick and restores them to health."

It's as equally important to use soap to wash off any residue. Lather from S.O.A.P is simply this, "Soaring Over Annoying People". Leave doubters and naysayers to their own opinions; bathe yourself in the wisdom and presence of God. In the Book of John 13:10 it reads, "Jesus replied, a person who has bathed all over does not need to wash, except for the feet, to be entirely clean." What Jesus is letting us know here is to shake the dust off your feet and continue to walk by faith. I can bear witness to what that means in my own life. I have been overlooked, misunderstood, talked about, even ridiculed many times because what I believe is right. So, you must with all sincerity, keep a positive outlook on your future.

When you think about missed opportunities, there are a few things to consider:

1. Thoughts - you must internalize your thoughts to align with how God thinks about you.
2. Educate - be responsible to utilize the information given to you during your decision-making process.
3. Alignment - all things will come together as the anointing which is upon your life enables the proper resources to be deposited for your purpose.
4. Manifestation - God will enlarge your capacity as the plan is being revealed for your life to unleash opportunity and increase.

When all of these principles are implemented the right way, at the right time, then there will be no more missed opportunities. I know you might be saying, "It's easier said than done"; I encourage you to receive this perspective as a viewpoint that can be accomplished. When you read Philippians 1:6 (NLT), "And I am certain that God, who began the good work until it is finally finished on the day when Christ Jesus returns." You see a completely awesome revelation as a reminder that, what you have started will not be left undone. You shall catapult as a result of what you thought was a missed opportunity.

Many people across the world are looking at themselves with this same thought pattern and asking questions; did I do something wrong? Why didn't my idea work? The answer to these questions is adversity leads to opportunity. If you did not try, how would you know the power of God? The beauty of it is the fact that you tried, and because of this, your faith is stronger. You have more wisdom and a better understanding of what it takes to overcome setbacks.

What we must begin to understand is that the Body of Christ needs more established and mature mentors so the kingdom process will function in full measure, according to the biblical patterns that God has placed on the earth. Let your faith move into skyrocket mode. Take off the limits and stay focused through hard work. Everything you're striving for will pay off.

This is your season of determination, and to become an unstoppable force for greatness. You may have had some missed opportunities, but you are more talented now than ever before. Reach up, roll up your sleeves and get to work! Move with passion and purpose to your desired goals. Make a list of priorities and keep things in order. This is considered a consistent spiritual check-up pertaining to your attitude, mind, health, progress and relationships. You must remain balanced in all aspects of your life.

There are multiple things that are impacted with your decisions. For example, your integrity, character and willingness are essential for these moves to come to pass. Missed opportunities are designed to enhance your development.

As you get older, these wisdom truths will stick with you. Talk with people who can mentor and advise a strategy, based upon their experience to overcome shortfalls and bad situations. They have an abundance of information to share, if you choose to receive.

These people come into your life at critical times for a reason. God does not desire for you to miss any more opportunities, especially when there's so much greatness that you must tap into. Write a vision and see it through until you reach the potential of those opportunities. There will be more to come. You will have the wisdom to prevent missed opportunities.

CHAPTER 2

NAVIGATING THROUGH NEGATIVE SYSTEMS

In this chapter, we will discuss the word 'negative'. Why are there so many underlying perceptions to the word 'negative'? I believe that it is possible to change the narrative for a positive outcome from something that was negative. So, as you navigate through negative situations, take the opportunity to grab wisdom and understanding for better solutions.

Negative:

1. Consisting in, or characterized by the absence, rather than the presence of distinguishing features.
2. A person, attitude, or situation not desirable or optimistic.
3. Of a quantity less than zero; to be subtracted from others or from zero.
4. Of, containing, producing, or denoting the kind of electric charge carried by electrons.

Systems:

1. A set of things working together as part of a mechanism, or an interconnecting network.
2. A set of principles, or procedures according to which something is done, an organized scheme or method.
3. The prevailing political or social order, especially when regarded as oppressive and intransigent.
4. A set of staves (plural for staff) in a musical score joined by a brace.

In our society today, there are so many systems that impact us from a negative perspective. One must ask themselves, 'what can I do to produce positivity versus negativity in my life'? Proverbs 15:3 reads "The eyes of the Lord are everywhere, keeping watch on the wicked and the good." God is watching over everything that will occur in your life.

Social media is considered a system of communication. Whether bad or good, this system interconnects people from all generations; therefore, other systems begin to fade and are not as useful in times past. As you continue to broaden your way of thinking, put systems in place that are going to stimulate growth and prosperity. If you're an entrepreneur, your goal is to build your company so it can increase your revenue. Many people have the habit of seeing things negatively instead of the opposite. Because of this mentality, they fail to navigate through negative systems.

Think about when you're facing challenges of every kind; the last thing you need is for someone to keep reminding you of how you did not complete your task. Whether it is paying your bills on time or finishing a college degree, you must hold yourself to a higher standard than what a system will think of you.

Now systems are a guide to having a practical approach to success and all that comes with success. In order to reach the potential of the success, you must overcome the stereotypes that exist. The Bible states in Psalm 81:13-14 "If my people would only listen to me, if Israel would only follow my ways, how quickly I would subdue their enemies and turn my hand against their foes!" This is a powerful statement and should encourage you to know that God has your back.

In my faith walk with God, I have learned, in several situations, to remove my own ideas or logic about how things should turn out. In retrospect, I quickly realized that the negative systems were not designing to end all or be all. They were educational experiences about my life's ambitions and dreams. The time we are experiencing right now, we must know God has a yearning to see us become successful, as it is the will of God for our lives.

There are some alarming statistics, from different polls, that were taken as a consensus in the United States; 59% of the American population live paycheck to paycheck. Another poll indicates that 1 in 17 Americans, based upon demographics and resources, do not have suitable healthcare and life insurance to cover expenses if they were to die. There must be solutions to these issues; many of the systemic resources have failed through policy and politics in our country. This type of negligence is normal for most poverty-stricken neighborhoods and families.

I propose that there is a better way; however, many Americans, who trusted in governmental leadership to solve these problems, have lost confidence in the elected officials because of money, power-driven greed and capitalism.

In 1 Chronicles 29:14-15 it says, "But who am I, and who are my people, that we should be able to give generously as this? Everything comes from you, and we have given you only what comes from your hand. We are foreigners and strangers in your sight, as were all of our ancestors. Our days on the earth are like a shadow, without hope." When you're navigating through negative systems, it's so easy to lose hope if there is no plan for success. I believe that one dynamic is how people are treated from a negative experience.

This type of behavior each day from customer services, bank tellers, hospital visits, school systems, and especially the political arenas are seen often. There is a direct impact of negativity and you ask the question, "How are we going to come through this?" The answer is in the Word of God. Jeremiah 29:11 reads "For I know the plans I have for you," declares the Lord, "plans to prosper you and not harm you, plans to give you hope and a future." Every adversity is an opportunity for something awesome to take place to make life better.

A strategy is necessary for your dreams to come alive; you must remain dedicated to make every moment count. As a person who has dedicated my life to serving others, I am an advocate to see people living their best life. However, there are many people who refuse to have confidence and trust in the process, so anxiety takes over the mind. I have witnessed people who are extremely motivated and focused for real change in their circumstances and change happens almost immediately.

Look at the parable Jesus spoke in Mark 4:26-29, "He also said, this is what the kingdom of God is like. A man scatters seed on the ground. Night and day, whether he sleeps or gets up, the seed sprouts and grows, though he does not know how. All by itself, the soil produces grain - first the stalk, then the head, then the full kernel in the head. As soon as the grain is ripe, he puts the sickle to it, because the harvest has come."

As we close this chapter, remember, navigating through negative systems can be challenging, but accomplished. If you take all of the tools from your experiences and utilize the wisdom, knowledge, and information given to you, then you will be able to navigate, sustain, direct, and create the joyous outcomes you desire.

CHAPTER 3

SCHOOL IS IN SESSION

Education is the gateway to success, and the love of learning helps to develop your core components to becoming stabilized in uncertain times. There must be premium instructions given to individuals who have dreams and plans for a great life. You say, how do I get there? The answer is simple! You must attend a school that will catapult your talents, gifts and skills through education and mentoring.

School - Educate:

1. An institution for educating children
2. Any institution at which correction is given in a discipline
3. A group of people, particularly writers, artists, or philosophers, sharing the same or similar ideas, methods, or style

A school is an educational institution designed to provide learning spaces and learning environments for instruction given to students, under the direction of teachers. Most countries have systems of formal education, which are commonly compulsory. In these systems, students' progress through a series of schools.

The names for these schools vary by country, but generally include primary school for young children and secondary school for teenagers who have completed their primary education. An institution where higher education is taught, is commonly called a college, or university, but these higher education institutions are usually not compulsory. According to data released by the

Department of Education, graduation rates in the United States are up from 84.1 percent in 2016 to 84.6 percent in 2017. On another note, according to Forbes magazine, as of June 06, 2018, America has a college dropout problem. The four-year completion rate —that is, the share of students who complete a bachelor's degree in the time the program is expected to take, is just 28 percent. This is an outrageous statistic to see, and now, having the opportunity to assimilate with young people as a private school educator,

I am disturbed by the trends I have experienced from the conversations I frequently have with all age demographics. There is a societal epidemic that has swept across America, where education is not a priority to most of the millennial generation. The focus has become more about money, fame, and popularity amongst peers and socialists alike on several social media platforms. It has become so apparent today to some, that education is not needed in order to establish success in your life.

I believe this is an illusion and trick of the enemy through greed, fame, and manipulation.

This approach has truly taken a stronghold on the younger minds of today.

The Bible declares to us in Hosea 4:1-6, "Hear the word of the Lord, you Israelites, because the Lord has a charge to bring against you who live in the land: There is no faithfulness, no love, no acknowledgment of God in the land. There is only cursing, lying and murder, stealing and adultery; they break all bounds, and bloodshed follows bloodshed. Because of this, the land dries up, and all who live in it waste away; the beasts of the field, the birds in the sky and the fish of the sea are swept away. But let no one bring a charge and let no one accuse another; for your people are like those who bring charges against a priest. You stumble day and night, and the prophets stumble with you. So, I will destroy your mother. My people are destroyed for lack of knowledge."

When you begin to analyze and put things in proper perspective, you will see many open holes that are in our society and in the church. I remember growing up in a very impoverished neighborhood in a very small town. The emphasis of education was personified because it was the only way out of the neighborhood. It was that or joining the military.

I was able to witness many from my neighborhood joining the ranks of the military; they would come back home in their uniforms, including my uncle; there was a sense of belonging and achievement. I wanted nothing more than to finish school and join the military myself, because to me, it was the only way out of my situation. Feeling the anguish of defeat because of the lack of opportunities, and no one setting a true example of education, I decided that I needed to step up. I saw too many people, family and friends mostly, who were not trying to establish their mark on a society where things were in peril, and desperation was inevitable.

This may be a current, or past place for many of you who are reading this book. I wanted so badly to do something great with my life; to possess meaning and satisfaction. So, I graduated from high school, enrolled in college and joined the military. I was extremely motivated by the despair of the neighborhood where I grew up, to avoid a life of crime, drugs, alcohol and much regret. I noticed it was time to embrace forward movement. Jesus said in Matthew 6:31-34, "So do not worry, saying, 'What shall we eat?' or 'What shall we drink?' or 'What shall we wear?' For the pagans run after all these things, and your heavenly Father knows that you need them. But seek first His kingdom and His righteousness, and all these things will be given to you as well. Therefore, do not worry about tomorrow, for tomorrow will worry about itself. Each day has enough trouble of its own."

Twenty-eight years later, I retired from the United States Army, achieved four degrees, and nine certifications. You must apply what you have learned along the way. I encourage you to read the Word of God and apply what is necessary in each season of life. You will see results in real-time, as long as God is in control. Life lessons do not come to destroy you, but to strengthen you when things look bleak. We live in a very progressive culture today, and from a standpoint where people question the validity of the power of God. It all starts at home; the experiences of what young people are introduced to, through different gates that are open for them to enter. There are encrypted messages and undertones being released through demonic forces and portals. The access that many people have today is unlimited, and the devil will use all vehicles possible to travel into dark places.

This type of access is very frantic and alarming. I am constantly on guard for my own children, nieces, and nephews. Questions must be asked by parents, teachers, caregivers and mentors to help guide this young generation into all truths. From where I stand, I see a lack of influence to do what's right. These are conversations I am having with the young and old, without any semblance of understanding as to why they are taking this approach.

I recently completed a poll by interviewing my students, local customers at the barbershop, other colleagues, former military leaders and community leaders, as well as pastors. All of them have a consensus saying that "there is a problem and we need to educate".

Over 76% of the people I interviewed, stated that we live in a society of racism, bigotry, greed, selfishness, lies, deceit, and brokenness. They don't believe there is a path set up for them to succeed, whether it's attending school, serving in the military or being an entrepreneur. The question I propose is this; how do we break this stalemate thinking? I am a true supporter of education, an advocate for military service, and a mentor in business initiatives. But more importantly, I am a teacher of the gospel of Jesus Christ.

I petition many of you to attend some type of ministry school, at a time when it's necessary for you to receive better insight into the knowledge of God. The more you pattern your life in the direction that God has allowed, the more you will become empowered to do all things as the Lord gives you the strength. Never have animosity towards what you did not understand!

Many of us have experienced some type of neglect and erroneous teachings at a time in our journey. When we get older, we are supposed to do better; however, in this age of so much uncertainty, people are taking shortcuts as a normal way of life. How did the dreams and aspirations of life education become such a drag and many children, to include adults, frown upon the importance of schooling?

Responding to Moral Decay:

Since the late 1970s, homeschooling has experienced a phenomenal increase, and today an estimated 650,000 to 1,000,000 children are taught at home. Parents who homeschool desire a less structured environment, more control over what their children learn, and freedom to teach moral values. Though several critics would claim that children suffer from lack of social contact and quality instruction, studies show that homeschoolers achieve higher scores than most public-school students on achievement tests and college entrance exams.

In recent years, many state legislators have proposed a system of vouchers to provide parents with school choice programs and options. Parents are ultimately responsible for their children's education.

This can also be seen in ministry and the marketplace for career progression. Most people today are required to have some type of formal education for leadership positions in ministry. In some cases, there is a misstep that ends up placing people who are inadequate for servitude in such trusted positions. I have seen in the military, where a service member did not meet the prerequisite for specific positions and the standards get bypassed.

The result is that now you have someone with no credentials to support the actions required for such a position. In the marketplace, it's no different. You witness well-qualified individuals getting overlooked and never receiving an opportunity for an interview, but someone who's below the qualification radar gets the promotion. Makes you wonder, why is this happening?

Simply put, we have a society that is driven by popularity. What we need are standard bearers in the church, community, our cities and states, and especially our government. Let's get back to the basics of education so that a generation is not wasted on entertaining the spirit of illusion.

The Word of God says in 2 Thessalonians 2:3-4, "Don't let anyone deceive you in anyway, for that day will not come until the rebellion occurs and the man of lawlessness is revealed, the man doomed to destruction. He will oppose and exalt himself over everything that is called God or is worshiped, so that he sets himself up in God's temple, proclaiming himself to be God."

Deception:

1.   The action of deceiving someone
2.   A thing that deceives

We are in that time now, and this is why school is session.

CHAPTER 4

OVERCOMING
CONSPIRACY THEORIES

A conspiracy theory is an explanation of an event or situation that invokes a conspiracy — generally one involving an illegal or harmful act that is supposedly carried out by government or other powerful actors — without credible evidence.

Many unproven conspiracy theories exist with varying degrees of popularity, frequently related to clandestine government plans and elaborate murder plots. Conspiracy theories usually deny consensus, cannot be proven using the historical or scientific method and are not to be confused with research concerning verified conspiracies.

Many people believe conspiracy theories over the truth, according to statistics, social media, news outlets, television and movies. I believe that most people are infatuated with something that entertains them, rather than something that is going to bring wisdom.

Why is that? Partly because we live in such an indulgent society that focuses on getting the facts wrong instead of right. Teaching is needed because discernment is necessary. There is strong evidence of so many people being led astray through a channel of lies and deceit. The Word of God clearly states in 2 Timothy 2:17-18, "Their teaching will spread like gangrene. Among them are Hymenaeus and Philetus, who have departed from the truth. They say the resurrection has already taken place, and they destroy the faith of some."

Wow, this is powerful and relevant to so many situations that I have heard from several people.

I've noticed the subliminal messages that are displayed and portrayed in music and movies. Speaking with my own children, their friends, and many youths that I mentor and teach, it is a stark contrast from what my generation faced over thirty years ago. I am appalled at the lack of sensitivity that many people do not exemplify to empower someone else. This is outrageous and contradictive to what Jesus has shown in His parables.

Matthew 5:43-48 states, "You have heard that it was said, 'Love your neighbor and hate your enemy.' But I tell you, love your enemies and pray for those who persecute you, that you may be children of your Father in heaven. He causes his sun to rise on the evil and the good and send rain on the righteous and the unrighteous. If you love those who love you, what reward will you get? Are not even the tax collectors doing that? And if you greet only your own people, what are you doing more than others? Do not even pagans do that? Be perfect, therefore, as your heavenly Father is perfect."

You should never allow conspiracy theories to control the narrative of your life. God is all-knowing and sovereign for how His thoughts are concerning your purpose and plan. In order to really dive into the essence of what you are called to be, you must experience the encounters with God in a majestic way. I would like to introduce you to the God encounters:

1. Invitation:
    a. The act of inviting
    b. An often-formal request to be present or participate
    c. Incentive, inducement

    Luke 5:27-31, "After this, Jesus went out and saw a tax collector by the name of Levi, sitting at his tax booth. "Follow Me," Jesus said to him, and Levi got up, left everything and followed Him. Then Levi held a great banquet for Jesus at his house, and a large crowd of tax collectors and others were eating with them. But the Pharisees and the teachers of the law who belonged to their sect complained to his disciples, "Why do you eat and drink with tax collectors and sinners?" Jesus answered them, "It is not the healthy who need a doctor, but the sick. I have not come to call the righteous, but sinners to repentance."

Jesus is letting us know that He has come for one that was overlooked, not good enough, the one they thought could not succeed, and the one who is not smart enough. Those are the ones that conspiracy theorists seem to forget about. However, when you invite God into your situations and let Him lead the way, then you can overcome conspiracy theories.

2. Impartation:
    a. Make (information) known; communicate
    b. Bestow (a quality)
    c. Transmission of information-imparting
    d. To give, convey, or grant from, or as if from a store.

Impart and communicate to others with the final purpose to offer direction in which we should understand the social activity of the hierarchy, like imitation, impartation, participation, measure and unification.

Acts 9:10-16 states, "In Damascus, there was a disciple named Ananias. The Lord called to him in a vision, "Ananias!" "Yes, Lord," he answered. The Lord told him, "Go to the house of Judas on Straight Street and ask for a man from Tarsus named Saul, for he is praying. In a vision he has seen a man named Ananias come and place his hands on him to restore his sight." "Lord," Ananias answered, "I have heard many reports about this man and all the harm he has done to your holy people in Jerusalem. And he has come here with authority from the chief priests to arrest all who call on your name." But the Lord said to Ananias, "Go! This man is my chosen instrument to proclaim my name to the Gentiles and their kings and to the people of Israel. I will show him how much he must suffer for my name."

In this dispensation, in order to impact change, you need impartation from God. The Apostle Paul had to go through a conversion of his beliefs and his understanding about the people of Israel. This transformation could only come through impartation. His position was going to be scrutinized, all his past was now questioned and how it could be that God will use him to become an instrument of change. This means we are supposed to utilize what is given to us and galvanize the moment to bring truth to the narrative about Christ. That is why many individuals deal with conspiracy daily. They must take time to incorporate the necessary tools to help raise awareness about the injustices that happen all of the time.

In my own experiences, I am witnessing a growing concern about what is right and wrong. There are many people dealing with trials and tribulations of various kinds. They don't know where to turn and who they can trust. There are symptoms in such a time as this where change has come. The question is whether the people have an ear to hear. Listen to wisdom and information from impartation for their destination.

3. Revelation:
   a. A surprising and previously unknown fact, especially one that is made known in a dramatic way
   b. The making known of something that was previously secret or unknown
   c. Used to emphasize the surprising or remarkable quality of someone or something
   d. The divine or supernatural to humans of something relating to human existence or the world

e. An act of revealing or communicating divine truth

f. Something that is revealed by God to humans

g. An act of revealing to view or making known

h. Something that is revealed, especially an enlightening

1 Corinthians 2:6-10 states, "We do, however, speak a message of wisdom among the mature, but not the wisdom of this age or the rulers of this age, who are coming to nothing. No, we declare God's wisdom, a mystery that has been hidden and that God destined for our glory before time began. None of the rulers of this age understood it, if they had, they would not have crucified the Lord of glory. However, as it is written: "What eye has not seen, what ear has not heard, and what no human mind has conceived - the things God has prepared for those who love him

- these are the things God has revealed to us by His spirit. The Spirit searches all things, even the deep things of God."

There comes a time where taking a deep breath is the best therapy when you're striving to receive results from seeing the revelation of what God has shown you. If you make a choice, you can maneuver through situations and scenarios that are beneficial. Stress is a component of negative thinking, and most need some level of encouragement at different stages of their journey.

Take time for reflection and self-discovery; don't allow overwhelming conflicts to drive your emotions and decisions. There are plenty of problems and distractions that arise throughout your day-to-day activities. Therefore, give yourself time for adjustment to make an executive decision that will remove any undue penetrators that suppress your time, energy, and thinking.

Here are a few prophetic adjustments to enhance your revelation:

1. Exercise - activity requiring physical effort, carried out to sustain or improve health and fitness.
   - 2 Timothy 2:5-6 (NKJV) "And also, if anyone who competes in athletics, he is not crowned unless he competes according to the rules. The hardworking farmer must be first to partake of the crops."

2. Meditate - a discourse intended to express its author's reflection, or to guide others in contemplation.
   - Joshua 1:8 (NKJV) "This Book of the Law shall not depart from your mouth, but you shall meditate in it day and night, that you may observe to do according to all that is written in it. For then you

will make your way prosperous and then you will have good success."

3. Plan - a detailed proposal for doing or achieving something.

    ·   Psalm 25: 9(NKJV) "The humble He guides in justice. And the humble He teaches His way."

4. Write - compose (a text or work) for written or printed reproduction or publication: put into literary form and set down in writing.

    ·   Zechariah 4:9(NKJV) "The hands of Zerubbabel have laid the foundation of this temple. His hands shall also finish it. Then you know, that the Lord of hosts has sent Me to you."

5. Move - go in a specific direction or manner, change position. Make progress; develop in a particular manner or direction.

- Exodus 14:19(NKJV) "And the Angel of God, who went before the camp of Israel moved and went behind them, and the pillar of cloud went from before them and stood behind them."

Take these adjustments and utilize them to fullest of your ability and have faith to trust God through the process. You will see the blessing of the Lord make you rich and add no sorrow. I can truly testify to you, that even in my own life, I had to start from somewhere. I started from right where I was at that moment.

I encourage you today, as you are reading this chapter, see your finish line. You must get out of the starting block and finish your race. It does not matter if it's the 100-yard dash, or the 200-meter hurdles. When you hear "on your mark, get set, go", get off the blocks and run as hard as you can. One of the most important things to remember about professional runners is that they train for a very long time. They work on techniques, components, and different running styles. Along the way, they build muscular strength and endurance, because they know the journey is not going to be easy. To ensure success for the race, most of the runners are doing a lot of research and creating good habits for themselves that will give them confidence to compete, and not be injured. They learn from previous races; also from talking with other runners, joining running groups, and they train with world class sprinters who have a mindset to win.

Well, it's the same way with you and God. You must conversate with Him about the strategy, then afterwards, take and evaluate the plan, staying motivated to see it through to the end. This is a critical moment in your life. You can embrace the wisdom that is being shared to achieve the ultimate goal, according to the adjustments that you have made.

In conclusion, there must be a plan that enables you to begin with a power push. Pickup traction and speed as you continue to implement one strategy after the next. You're feeling great about what you've produced. Once this is underway, take a temporary pause and do a progress report to track your status. Finally, put away every malicious thought or idea. Remove all levels of frustration, holding onto what is positive and helpful, because you made it to the finish line by eliminating all conspiracy theories.

CHAPTER 5

YOUR LEGACY MEANS SOMETHING

Legacy - Something handed down from one generation to the next.

We live in a very progressive and accelerated society today. There are various distractions that are designed to interfere with your forward movement in life. The plan, or goal is to never get stuck, losing hope in your vision. Establishing a legacy for future generations is the utmost importance to prepare the foundation for generations to come. I encourage you to help those that are being raised up now to establish a precedent, leaving an imprint in the spirit of legacy.

> "The Lord will command the blessing on you in your storehouses and in all to which you set your hand, and He will bless you in the land which the Lord your God is giving you."
>
> -Deuteronomy 28:8 (NKJV)

Legacy is also a matter of what you desire for it to become. Plan and follow the instructions for consistency and production to build for the future of generations to come. Master your destiny with insight, drive, passion and discipline. These are the essential ingredients to build the foundation from the beginning. It's paramount to start your foundation with a solid outlook and build it accordingly. There is no need to try and emulate what someone else is doing. It may not work for you; this would be outside the limits of your sculpted foundation. I remember when

I was around fifteen years old, my Dad told me I needed a job. It was the beginning of summer and school was out, so I was preparing for high school. My dad told me, "You're coming to work with me today. Get up and let's go." I immediately put on some working clothes and hurried out the door. We got to the construction site and began pouring cement for the foundation. My father says to me, "In order to have a strong foundation, it takes time to level off the ground." To my surprise, I understood this revelation, and even until this day, I can still hear his voice speaking this to me.

Over the years, one thing that truly helped me was to stay with the task at hand. I learned early on in my youth to devote as much time and effort as possible to be successful at whatever I plan to achieve. Watching many older, successful people, taught me the value of hard work and integrity. As you look across the spectrum of your life and where you are trying to go, remember it takes hard work and integrity to get the job done.

In Psalm 119:105 the scripture says, "The Word of God is a lamp to my feet, and a light to my path." This is very profound in this time. The light represents sight. You can see where you are going. The limits have been taken because of darkness and blindness. However, there is a meaning of hope, and place of freedom. No more blockage is obstructing you from your legacy.

Let's look at the word 'light'.

Light is the natural agent that stimulates sight and makes things visible. It is also identified as understanding of a problem or mystery; to enlighten.

Knowing what you know now, you can understand the light. It is very significant to the chartered path you are on for the blessings God has waiting for you. Never let your trust waiver, because you are a lot closer to the legacy now than before.

I have been processing many things over the years, and I came to this conclusion; "You must have the desire to leave a legacy." I was speaking with my oldest son recently, and he said to me, "Dad, you are setting up a great legacy." I asked him what made him make this statement. He replied,

"I have watched you sacrifice so much for us, and I am grateful for what you have accomplished in your life." I must admit, I was humbled by his comments and it really encouraged me to keep going. I hope this scenario enlightens someone to keep going.

Everyone does not have IRAs, annuities, stocks and bonds, or money market accounts. Most of us are law-abiding citizens, who work jobs and have careers that give retirement options. Through this process, you pay insurance for your home, car, or health. Trying to put money in your savings account is an undaunting task, because of the cost of living and high inflation on everyday things you need. When you grow from nothing, and you're trying to establish something, it takes time and effort. Attending financial seminars and classes in accounting, record keeping, and financial investments are so important.

There are a few things to consider as you are building your legacy:

Dr. Fredrick J. Harris

1. Start a budget - this is one of the most efficient ways to establish financial discipline and independence.
   - Proverbs 3:9-10 - "Honor the Lord with your wealth, with the first fruits of your crops; then your barns will be filled to overflowing, and your vats will brim over with new wine."

2. Spend with discipline - monitoring what you spend and how you spend it are vital to obtaining financial gain towards your legacy.
   - Matthew 6:19 - "Do not store up for yourselves treasures on earth, where moths and vermin destroy, and where thieves break in and steal."

3. Invest in your future - take the opportunity to attend further schooling. Also, invest in a college fund program for your children.
   - Psalm 37:25-26 - "I was young and now I am old, yet I have never seen

> the righteous forsaken or their
> children begging bread. They are
> always generous and lend freely; their
> children will be a blessing."

Taking your investment life seriously is essential and paramount in this journey. Do an entire layout of the goals you plan to obtain, and as you do this, you will see yourself operating from a place of surplus, rather than a deficit. This type of approach is very difficult for many people, based upon never being exposed to such accountability in their life. You must have parameters that will only allow you to go so far and spend so much.

There was a program on the internet that I was watching; the discussion being about public school vs. private school. Where would you send your children for education? The conversation got very intense between the host and guests, because it became personal about the level of income with many people in America. The guest panelist stated, "Most people do not have a desire to become millionaires; they prefer to live comfortably without debt."

The host of the show did not agree with the comments and believed that many people want to become millionaires. I agreed with the guest panelist because in my own assessment, just looking at my life, I have a desire to remain comfortable with little to no debt, rather than becoming a millionaire. Just because a person is a millionaire, it does not guarantee happiness. Mark 8:36(NIV) says, "What good is it for someone to gain the whole world, yet forfeit their soul?"

Very interesting! You can see this behavior every day in our society. The promotion is owning businesses and is not striving towards having a notable career. All people do not want the same thing in life. Even if you have a difference of opinion, you can still be respectful of someone's decision to remain comfortable and not seek after riches and fame. My desire is to make an impact and leave a mark that can't be erased.

Now, my wife and I have taken the time to prepare our kids for college by establishing their college funds. We did not want them to struggle. We want things to be much easier for them in some areas. I took a broad look at my father's generation to understand their trials and struggles. This opened my eyes and my mind, to know I must prepare early if my children are going to have success, not only in education, but any pursuit of purpose they desire.

For some people, this may seem impossible to establish, so I normally say to anyone, "start from where you are". If you can focus on that nugget only, it will alleviate so much stress that falls upon your life. There are going to be peaks and valleys along the way; however, step by step, bit by bit, these goals can be achieved.

You will find yourself with more energy and satisfaction to know that the foundation has already been laid. You then start the journey of leaving a legacy that cannot be erased. Your legacy does not have to be approved by man, but God only. He is too awesome to allow you to walk around with self-pity because of things that happened outside of your control.

Destiny awaits you; there is an excitement in the atmosphere about the inheritance in front of you. I can truly say that "the best is yet to come". Focus on what you are obtaining and move with a boldness. Leave your children, grandchildren and great - grands in a better position than what you experienced coming up.

We must leap over every excuse and start to work towards the future. The person who does nothing, receives nothing. My prayer is that this person is not you, but you are open to the realization that you can accomplish your dreams and unlock purpose through doors of opportunity.

I'm reminded of a time while I was serving on active duty. I would always speak to my soldiers about finances and education. Very few of them had a plan to succeed and get promoted in the ranks. What I came to find out later, is that many soldiers come to the military with a mindset they grew up with. If I came from impoverished conditions, I would think with an impoverished attitude. When a soldier is recruited into the U.S. Army, they are given the opportunity to select a career field, or military occupational specialty. With this selection, based upon test scores, they can receive other incentives like a bonus, choice of duty, and other specialty schools and training.

They attend basic training and then move on to their advanced individual training to become certified in the career field of choice. This could not be possible had they kept the same mindset from their civilian life. When the soldier arrives at basic training, it begins. The drill instructor has the task of taking a civilian and turning them into a soldier. One of the first things they are told, "Forget everything you left behind; you are a part of a new family." This is the beginning of everything new for your life. So, you are fashioned into your future through training, teaching, coaching and mentoring. These elements are necessary for success in your legacy.

Philippians 3:12-14(NASB) says, "Not that I have already attained, or am already perfected; but I press on, that I may lay hold of that for which Christ Jesus has also laid hold on to me. Brethren, I do not count myself to have apprehended; but one thing I do, forgetting those things which are behind and reaching forward to those things which are ahead, I press toward the goal for the prize of the upward call of God in Christ Jesus."

It's time to move forward with your legacy. Here are a few principles to help along the way:

1. Training - the action of teaching a person, or animal, a skill or type of behavior.
2. Teaching - the occupation, profession, or work of a teacher. Ideas or principles taught by an authority.
3. Coaching - a form of development in which a person, called a coach, supports a learner or client in achieving a specific personal or professional goal.
4. Mentoring - advise or train (someone, especially a younger colleague).

I'm finding it more and more difficult to motivate the present generation these days. A lot of times, I find myself frustrated because they're not like my generation when it comes to drive and focus. However, over the last few years, I have become keenly aware that many of them do not take advantage of the opportunities given to them. Most of it has to do with the way many children are raised in the present age. A tremendous number of parents are overworked, have multiple jobs, the responsibility of more children, have underpaid employment, and several other factors that prevent the proper nourishment that children need in this hour.

From generation to generation there are a sleuth of things that were learned to bring growth and to establish a foundation. Unfortunately, the older generation has gotten tired and lethargic with passing along knowledge that would make this generation more successful. Instead, you see so much anger and infighting amongst families, friends, co-workers and even church members and leaders. There is a strong portal of apathy that has been opened; this generation has fallen into a deep sleep and needs to wake up.

Your legacy is supposed to mean something. Pass things down that will bring revelation, wisdom, honesty, and love.

CHAPTER 6

NO MORE COMPROMISE

To compromise is to make a deal between different parties, where each party gives up part of their demand. In arguments, compromise is a concept of finding agreement through communication, through mutual acceptance of terms, often involving variations from an original goal or desire. Let's look at the definition below.

Compromise - an agreement, or a settlement of a dispute that is reached by each side making concessions.

a. An ability to listen to two sides in a dispute and devise a compromise acceptable to both.

Synonyms - agreement

b. Settle a dispute by mutual concession.

c. Accept standards that are lower than is desirable.

d. Bring into disrepute, or danger by indiscreet, foolish, or reckless behavior.

It has become more evident that the word compromise means you're weak and people can run over you. This is not a true statement and does not represent what God would require of us in His word. The Bible declares in Matthew 18:19-20, "Again, truly, I tell you that if two of you on earth agree about anything they ask for, it will be done for them by my Father in heaven. For where two or three gather in my name, there am I with them."

What Jesus is letting us know is that compromise is good when it is done in His name. You must have the right covenant, partners in prayer, and support to get through rough times. However, if you are continuing to circle the wagons amongst unbelief, then there will always be strife and animosity to get anything done.

When I observe our government and elected officials over the years, I see so much division. Some lack empathy, and their power of the pursuit for wealth and prosperity leaves our country vulnerable. There is a great compromise for greed and selfish ambitions, and therefore, you see so many leaders in the government and corporate workplaces getting into trouble because of compromise.

When I observe things from the perspective of ministry, I have seen the spirit of compromise creep in and infiltrate churches, ministry leaders, congregations, and taken a stronghold over the personal lives of many people. This is a sad epidemic that has caused so many problems and circumstances upon people's lives. Much of this is from what many have learned over the years. You can't expect to be successful in certain areas if there hasn't been anyone to teach you through wisdom and knowledge. I believe there is a way for better situations; however, the essence of doing it God's way is a major challenge for many people. They use several excuses as to why there is not a strong relationship with God.

Family dynamics are critical, work relationships are serious, and oftentimes, fellowship in ministry is paramount. If there is some type of compromise that is causing you to be broken, defeated, angry and frustrated all of the time, then, you must know it is time for a change. It must be done immediately. If these types of compromises are constantly overlooked, then before you know it, several years would have gone by and you will find yourself in the same condition all over again. If there is no healing, from past compromising dilemmas and bringing closure to episodes that have been lingering in and out of your life for decades, how are you going to be ready for the greater?

I've learned some very poignant principles along my life's journey, and I became increasingly more aware of things that were causing me more harm than good. To address the negative events, I surrounded myself with people who knew more than I did. I was able to manage different stressors, at certain times, by allowing those individuals to teach me things I was having trouble understanding. It was several situations that taught me humility and wisdom. So, here are a few things to consider about the law of compromise:

1. Appreciate Mature Relationships - it is vitally important to maintain these relationships to keep you accountable and transparent.

2. Negativity Leads to Deception - this way of compromise will cause a detrimental impact to your growth. You will become guilty by association.

3. Trust in Reliable Sources - whenever you are receiving information, before you say yes, ensure the source is reliable.

4. Fact Check Everything - no more deception or believing lies. It's important to know the facts instead of make-believe illusions.

5. Do Proper Closure - before you involve yourself with any more compromise, allow them to show consistency over a window of time. If they cannot deliver on their promise, you should not remain open to compromise.

Motivate yourself, and be encouraged, that you learned value principles for the prevention of setbacks. Your life is more than just a temporary compromise for a short victory, with no sustenance for the journey ahead. When you look in the Bible, in the book of Exodus, God kept the children of Israel moving without compromising. He showed them love, compassion, provision, chastisement, protection, wisdom and grace. Why did God continue to do this for them? Because, He loved them so much that compromise would have caused them to miss the opportunity for the glory to appear. Every time they had a need, the glory appeared unto them. You might be thinking, "I'm in this wilderness alone" and that is not the case. There are many others who are dealing with certain things that can cause a compromise. You want to improve in every aspect of your intended purpose. The steps you take toward redemption will give way to great results. Ponder these principles for thought:

A. What have I sacrificed? - think about what you have sacrificed, and how it will best serve you to change directions now for redemption.

B. Have a Bounce Back Mindset - demonstrate the faith to get rejuvenated for a comeback.

C. A Spirit of Resiliency - the more strength you have for victory, the easier things will be to handle.

D. The Zeal to Remain Tenacious - in this approach, you already understand what it will take to be great.

E. Rally the Troops of Encouragement -assemble yourself in a coalition of allies that really know how to encourage.

F. A Strategy for Success - pick the brain of successful people and ask the question that is never asked.

G. Seek Revelation - rely on the wisdom of God to enhance your revelation for clarity.

H. Pray for Sustainment - you must have the stamina to stay focused until you see results.

I. Remain Quiet - in order to fully receive the instructions, it takes great discipline to remain quiet in your secret place.

J. Limit Your Conversations - do not discuss too much of your plans openly, because something, or someone, could impede your growth.

K. Ask for Advice - never allow pride to keep you from asking the right questions at the right time. This will help with periodic assessments to stay on track.

L. Take a Progressive Approach - never be afraid of a challenge. This will help your faith to be stretched beyond your limits.

M. Be Ready for a Right - Now Moment - when your moment strikes, receive it with gladness and build upon it.

N. Never Neglect Small Victories - embrace small victories with a spirit of gratefulness. So, when larger victories come, you're not surprised.

O. Challenge Your Greatness - always think two levels ahead of where you currently are. Spend time in a position that you see yourself capturing at the right time.

P. Trust the Process - work through any distractions, enablers and stumbling blocks that come to slow your progress.

Q. Read about Statistics and Trends - survey your landscape to ensure that what you are working on can bring a reward immediately to enhance your future ambitions.

R. Stay Away from Procrastinators - never indulge in unfruitful conversations and times of idleness with people, places or things. This will limit your scope of production.

S. Prepare Your Proposals - as you are establishing a legacy, remember to have documentations for your entire roadmap for success. Keep everything in a safe location.

T. Design your Destiny - write the vision of your story and how you will tell it.

U. Master Your Talents - become superior at the skills and expertise you have accumulated along the way.

V. Exercise a Time of Meditation - the rigors of life can be overwhelming, so you must have time to reflect and relax.

W. Reposition Yourself - maximize what is consistent and lose what is hindering the next level. Always take the opportunity to reposition where you are headed.

X. Make a Bold Move - after you have aligned your thoughts and adjusted, take the leap of faith with boldness to accomplish your task at hand.

Y. Dream Big - dream like there is no tomorrow and activate a champion spirit from within.

Z. Keep Your Swagger - you are in motion for long-term success and stability. It's important to be able to connect with each generation and the dynamics that accompany them. Remain in touch with upgrades in technology, social media, people, community and society. They will become beneficial to you without compromise. You are there to make an impact, not create chaos.

We must be ready and willing to go the distance. It's imperative that your outlook is going to change the course of destiny. The only responsibility that many of us have is to make a difference, leaving everything better then when we received it. I learned this very important perspective while serving in the military. We were taught several wisdom keys to point us in a direction to make life better for ourselves and those around us.

Leadership is so important in this time of uncertainty. Our culture and way of living has been challenged by several goliaths. They have run rampant among God's people and must be confronted and exposed. What we need are some David's, with the heart of the Father to be fearless in battle and destroy Goliath. The Bible says in 1 Samuel 17:44-45(GNT), "Come on," he challenged David, "and I will give your body to the birds and animals to eat." David answered, "You are coming against me with sword, spear, and javelin, but I come against you in the name of the Lord Almighty, the God of the Israelite armies, which you have defied."

I believe that the reason why we have seen so many leadership challenges, in various areas of life, is due to the lack of accountability and oversight that were not established in the proper protocols. This will lead to a natural and spiritual malnutrition of people because of the lack of wisdom being displayed in politics, churches, corporations, law enforcement, medical clinics, professional sports, media and a whole host of others, with no barrier for conduct and behavioral standards.

James 1:3-5(GNT) states, "For you know that when your faith succeeds in facing such trials, the result is the ability to endure. Make sure that, without failing, so that you may be perfect and complete, lacking nothing. But if any of you lack wisdom, you should pray to God, who will give it to you; because God gives generously and graciously to all."

LEADERSHIP - the action of leading a group of people or an organization.

Synonyms: guidance – direction -authority – control - management – headship – directorship

- The state, or position, of being a leader
- The leaders of an organization, country, etc.

The military is one of the more, if not the top, example of leadership at multiple levels. The structure can influence and direct organizations and echelons to be in sync with direction, based upon the authority to respond and react to movement. The level of control from a stated position of authoritative help gives confidence to commanders and soldiers to accomplish the mission. Through training and rehearsals, the military has always put service members in a position of success and not compromise; that is why leadership is utterly essential when faced with a difficult task.

The Army lives by what is known as the Seven Army Values. These core values help to mold and shape a soldier to become fit and vigilant to accomplish their mission, living out these values. I like to use this model in the component of ministry and life, and I have used these core values to emulate growth and consistency in my daily life.

Ten Core Values of Leadership:

L= Loyalty - what areas of life are you loyal in your responses and reactions?

E= Endurance - where does the faith of endurance come from to keep you going forward?

A= Action - how do you act amid a crisis?

D= Duty - do you have a duty and obligation to compromise?

E= Educate - where does your education take over when there are setbacks?

R= Reinvent - how does someone reinvent after troubled times?

S= Speak - do you speak with confidence or frustration when nothing has changed?

H= Hope - how can I hang on to hope when there has been no fruit for my sacrifice?

I= Integrity - what is the strategy to keep my integrity intact without compromise?

P= Personal Courage/Protect - when do I exercise personal courage in order to overcome what I am lacking? How do I protect my vision in this process?

Seven Army Values are:

'LDRSHIP – Leadership'

Loyalty

Duty

Respect

Selfless Service

Honor

Integrity

Personal Courage

Leadership is defined as:

1. Vision - Leading means having a vision and sharing it with others.

2. Motivation - The leader knows how to motivate better than what an individual has been receiving in previous times.

3. Serving - The leader is at the service of the people, team, and organization.

4. Empathy - One of the basic and essential qualities of any leader.

5. Train - A leader trains individuals and groups to become great while mastering their craft.

In summary, there cannot be any more compromise to make it to where God desires for you to be. Go with boldness so you can see results and not illusions. I learned to trust God, no matter what came my way. It took a lot of time to train my thoughts, and understanding to come into full alignment with the plan of God. I had to suffer through many things in my life; I became more determined to win and to not fail. I removed everything that I knew was going to hinder me and my objective victory and came to a place of wisdom, so there would be no more compromise!

CHAPTER 7

THE WARRIOR BLUEPRINT

Whether it's utilizing weapons or hand-to-hand combat, the term 'warrior' is an identification of strength, power and fortitude to conquer. As a warrior, you have the capability to achieve success, never relenting your position because you are battle-tested. Great fighters train feverishly, conditioning their bodies and minds for whatever challenges they may face. The warrior in you must rise to the occasion and defeat the opposition.

Warrior: A person specializing in combat or warfare, especially within the context of tribal or clan-based warrior culture society that recognizes a separate warrior class or caste.

Types of Warriors:

Soldier

Knight

Samurai

Ninja

Cossacks

Mercenary

Fighter

Merchant

Worker

Warrior is defined as:

- A person engaged, or experienced, in warfare; broadly; a person engaged in some struggle or conflict.
- A person who shows, or has shown, great vigor, courage or aggressiveness for victory and triumph.

- Warrior - (especially in former times) a brave or experienced soldier or fighter.
- Warrior - Any of several standing poses in yoga, in which the legs are held apart and the arms are stretched outwards.

Serving in combat and engaging an enemy of hostile intent is very serious and life-threatening. I served on two combat tours to Iraq, and one tour to Afghanistan. I was up and close with enemy fighters in small arms fire exchanges, as well as being engaged by a car bomb (VBIED — Vehicle Borne Improvised Explosive Devices).

In 2005, I was on my second deployment to Iraq, and on this very hot day in the summer of July, I was keenly aware of the significance of the events taking place in the city of Baghdad and the country of Iraq. It was Election Day and we were on high alert because of suspected enemy activity. I walked outside and discerned something was not right. I approached my Commander and requested permission to go to the Entry Control Point (ECP) to check with the Iraqi soldiers to ensure everything was going well with their force protection.

I asked my counterpart to walk out to the gate with me. To our surprise, it looked like everything was going as planned. Then, all of a sudden, everything changed, and a vehicle entered the compound very slowly. I immediately repositioned our combat vehicles for extra protection and pointed the weapons strategically in the directions necessary to cover all sectors of fire.

The vehicle stopped and then began moving again. I raised my hand to motion for it to stop, but what happened next was not anything I would have expected. The driver stepped on the gas and sped toward our location. I reacted by engaging the car with my weapon, shooting out the windows, while trying to disable the vehicle. The driver was slouching down in his seat and continued in our direction. My counterpart began to move the Iraqi soldiers to safety behind the wall barriers to ensure if any type of explosion would erupt, that they would be protected from shrapnel.

As I continued to engage the vehicle, it slammed into one of the tanks. I ran to the passenger side and noticed that the bomber had his hand on the detonator. I shouted to everyone to get back, to seek cover because the car was about to blow. Within seconds the car exploded, and I landed approximately 20 meters away with shrapnel wounds and cuts all over my body.

I leapt to my feet and regained my composure in order to assess the situation. By then, there had been two blasts from this vehicle, but the big one was still to come. I noticed there were civilians walking toward the mosque for prayer. I ran over to them and escorted them to behind the wall barriers to reframe from injury. Then the third blast happened and blew a section of the wall out from in front of us.

The driver had then died, and the car was on fire. That was the signal for the small arms fire to begin. I directed the soldiers to flank to the front side to protect the gaping hole in the entry control point so no other vehicles could enter. Along with a group of soldiers, we moved to the outer corridor of the compound to engage enemy fire, taking out any other insurgent attack that would come our way. We were able to re-establish our perimeter and set up fortified barriers for any future attacks on our compound.

As a warrior, you must stay alert to stay alive! This is not the only context in a real-world situation, but also in the spirit realm. There are fights that take place and are designed to stretch your faith and your revelation to understand how God is moving in your favor to victory.

With this knowledge in mind, the Word of God is conducive to help establish your strength as a warrior; also, to know how to fight in combat, both naturally and spiritually. 2 Chronicles 18:29-32 (AMP) the king of Israel said to Jehoshaphat, "I will disguise myself and will go into battle, but you put on your 'royal' robes." So, the king of Israel disguised himself and they went into the battle. Now the king of Aram (Syria) had commanded the captains of his chariots, saying, "Do not fight with the small or the great, but only with the king of Israel."

So, when the captains of the chariots saw Jehoshaphat (of Judah), they said, "It is the king of Israel!" So, they turned to fight against him, but Jehoshaphat called out (for God's help), and the LORD helped him; and God diverted them away from him. When the captains of the chariots saw that it was not the king of Israel, they turned back from pursuing him."

There are a few principles to implement as the warrior who fights:

1. Anoint Your Hands - Psalm 144:1(NLT) "Praise the Lord, who is my rock. He trains my hands for war and gives my fingers skill for battle."

2. Put the Whole Armor of God - Ephesians 6:10-11(ESV) "Finally, be strong in the Lord and the strength of His might. Put on the whole armor of God, that you may be able to stand against the schemes of the devil period."

3. Sharpen Your Sword - 1 Samuel 17:51(KJV) "Therefore David ran, and stood upon the Philistine, and took his sword, and drew it out of the sheath thereof, and slew him, and cut off his head therewith. And when the Philistines saw their champion was dead, they fled."

4. Maintain Your Warrior Mentality - Romans 8:35-39(NASB) "Who will separate us from the love of Christ? Will tribulation, or distress, or persecution, or famine, or nakedness, or peril, or sword? Just as it is written, "FOR YOUR SAKE WE ARE PUT TO DEATH ALL DAY LONG; WE WERE CONSIDERED AS SHEEP TO BE SLAUGHTERED. But in all things, we overwhelmingly conqueror through Him who loved us. For I am convinced that neither death, nor life, nor angels, nor principalities, nor things present, nor things to come, nor powers, nor height, nor depth, nor any other created thing

will be able to separate us from the love of God, which is in Christ Jesus our Lord."

a. Mentality is - mental power or capacity

b. Mentality is - mood or way of thought

c. Mentality is - the characteristic attitude

d. Mentality is - capacity of intelligent thought

Warriors move in silence, leaving no detection that they were ever there. Many times, as believers, we must not allow several conversations to veer us off course from the original goal in mind. With this in mind, you can't afford the noise on the outside to penetrate the wisdom on the inside.

Ponder this scripture:

> "But when you do a charitable deed, do not let your left hand know what your right hand is doing. That your charitable deed may be in secret; and your Father who sees in secret will Himself reward you openly."
>
> -Matthew 6:3-4 (NKJV)

Warriors have the distinction like a police SWAT (Special Weapons and Tactics) team: a special section of some law enforcement agencies, trained and equipped to deal with an especially dangerous or violent situation, as when hostages are being held (often used attributively).

This is where warriors for the Lord are needed. You must be strong and courageous to fight for your miracles and success that only comes from God. If you will continue to let Him order your steps, God will provide for you in a great and powerful way. Prosperity is available and you must be strong, courageous, mindful, patient, prudent and organized.

"In the same way I was with Moses, I will be with you. I won't give up on you; I won't leave you. Strength! Courage! You are going to lead this people to inherit the land I promise to give their ancestors. Give it everything you have, heart and soul. Make sure you carry out The Revelation that Moses commanded you, every bit of it. Don't get off track, either left or right, to make sure you get to where you're going. And don't for a minute let this Book of The Revelation be out of mind. Ponder and meditate on it day and night, making sure you practice everything written in it. Then you'll get where you're going; then you'll succeed. Haven't I commanded you? Strength! Courage! Don't be timid; don't get discouraged. GOD, you're God, is with you every step you take." -Joshua 1:6-9 (MSG)

Philippians 4:13-19 (NIV) states, "I can do all this through Him who gives me strength. Yet it was good of you to share in my troubles. Moreover, as you Philippians know, in the early days of your acquaintances with the gospel, when I set out from Macedonia, not one church shared with me in the matter of giving and receiving, except you only; for even when I was in Thessalonica, you sent me aid more than once when I was in need. Not that I desired your gifts; what I desired is that more be credited to your account. I have received full payment and have more than enough. I am amply supplied, now that I have received, Epaphroditus, the gifts you sent, they are a fragrant offering, and acceptable sacrifice, pleasing to God. And my God will meet all your needs according to the riches of His glory in Christ Jesus.

The strength you carry is of boldness and power. This is not your time to cave into the pressure, but to make the mandate to go forward and not look back. As you do this, confrontation will come; so, do not take your eyes off the prize. Continue to trust the process."

And, Philippians 3:12-14 (AMP) states, "Not that I have already obtained it (this goal of being Christ-like) or have already been made perfect, but I actively press on so that I may take hold of that (perfection) for which Christ Jesus took hold of me and made me His own. Brothers and sisters, I do not consider that I have made it my own yet; but one thing I do: forgetting what lies behind and reaching forward to what lies ahead, I press on toward the goal to win the (heavenly) prize of the upward call of God in Christ Jesus."

Few things to consider:

1. Never Quit - Go the distance until the end. (Jeremiah 29:11)

2. Never Accept Defeat - Isaiah 54:17 (No weapon that is formed)

3. Never Leave Anyone Behind - Galatians 4:21-31

4. Warriors Always Lead by Example - Daniel 6:19-23

5. Train to Fight - Luke 6:40

6. Study to Learn - 2 Timothy 2:14-15

7. Start Fresh and Finish Strong - Philippians 1:6

The warrior blueprint is daunting and challenging, but achievable through God as you build your foundation on trust, wisdom, grace and love. God will provide whatever you need when you need it. There is great significance to what you are building, and it must be protected at all cost. Stand strong on the principles and the elements from your strategy. The power of God shall come upon you to bring liberation and freedom. Take a ride with God through prayer, worship and understanding. As you are taking flight, the Lord will guide you with his eye, so you'll see the warrior blueprint through the eyes of understanding.

> "I will instruct you and teach you in the way you should go; I will guide you with My eye."
>
> -Psalm 32:8 (NKJV)

> "I pray that the eyes of your heart may be enlightened in order that you may know the hope to which He has called you, the riches of His glorious inheritance in His holy people."
>
> -Ephesians 1:18 (NIV)

CHAPTER 8

SUCCESS IS MY DESTINY

As you continue to trust God and walk by faith, you will come to understand that you have a destiny. A person who walks with God will always get to their destination. In this hour of significance concerning where you are going, create a plan of action and establish a glide path that will give you a vantage point to arrive at your destination on time.

Success - the accomplishment of an aim or purpose.

Synonyms: favorable outcome (successfulness), prosperity - prosperousness, triumph, bestseller, results

- The attainment of popularity or profit.
- A person or thing that achieves desired aims or attains prosperity.

One of the most important factors to achieving success in life is to know the meaning of success for your personal life. The meaning of success goes far beyond wealth, fame and good looks. Here is one statistic to ponder: success is 1% inspiration and 99% perspiration, which means it takes a lot of hard work to achieve success. There are several ways to identify the meaning of success. Below are a few to consider:

Success defined by the mentality of the recipient:

A. Graduating high school
B. Completing a science project for a good grade

C.   Completing a degree in college

D.   Cooking a great meal

E.   Getting married and starting a family

F.   Start a business to become an entrepreneur

G.   Working as a youth counselor

H.   Running a marathon

This is just to name a few because there are so much more to define what being successful is all about. I believe what is going on in this generation of technology-driven success is their distortions of the truth. You have a generation of people that think, if you do not fit a certain status quo, then you will not be successful. Well, it all depends on your definition of what success means to you and your life. When I think about my own life and what God has allowed me to obtain, I consider myself successful in the eyes of the Lord. Someone else may look at success in another manner and that is totally ok, because everyone is entitled to their own opinions and insight to believe what they choose to believe.

Success:

Consider this: success in life is not based on what you can do, but what God can do for you and through you to bless others.

There is an application through the Word: Joshua 1:7(NASB) reads, "Be strong and very courageous; be careful to do according to all the law which Moses my servant commanded you; do not turn from it to the right or to the left, so that you may have SUCCESS wherever you go."

Destiny: what happens in the future - the things that someone or something will experience in the future; a power that is believed to control what happens in the future.

Destiny - A person's destiny is everything that happens to them during their life, including what will happen in the future, especially when it is controlled by someone or something beyond human element.

1. The things that will happen in the future.
2. The force that some people think controls what happens in the future and is outside human control.

3. The state of a person or thing in the future, considered as supernatural.

Scriptures to ponder or consider:

Psalm 25:8 (NKJV) – "The humble He guides in justice. And the humble He teaches His way."

Psalm 119:105 (NKJV) – "Your word is a lamp to my feet and a light to my path."

Jeremiah 12:5 (NKJV) - "If you have run with the footmen, and they wearied you, then how can you contend with the horses? And if in the land of peace, in which you trusted, they wearied you, then how will you do in the floodplain of the Jordan?"

Jeremiah 29:10-11(NKJV) – "For thus says the Lord: After seventy years are completed at Babylon, I will visit you and perform My good word toward you and cause you to return to this place. For I know the thoughts that I think toward you, says the Lord, thoughts of peace and not evil, to give you a future and a hope."

Matthew 6:33 (NKJV) - "But seek first the kingdom of God and His righteousness, and all these things shall be added to you."

John 14:1(NKJV) - "Let not your heart be troubled; you believe in God, believe also in Me."

2 Corinthians 5:7-8 (NKJV) - For we walk by faith, and not by sight. We are confident, yes, well pleased rather to be absent from the body and to be present with the Lord."

Take on the frame of mind that you cannot afford for your destiny to be washed away. You're at a critical turn in your destiny and it's time for success from all aspects. Go after the things that will help you prosper and move forward with power and wisdom.

Ponder this declaration: "Don't Wash Away My Destiny".

You have the glory, no need to worry...

The prophetic word always sets you in a posture for success!

God plants His prophetic word deep inside of you as a seed, so he can reap His harvest of what you were called and created to do in the earth.

GENESIS 2:5-8 (NIV) reads, "When the Lord God made the earth and the heavens, neither wild plants nor grains were growing on the earth. For the Lord God had not yet sent rain to water the earth, and there were no people to cultivate the soil. Instead, springs came up from the ground. He breathed the breath of life into man's nostrils, and the man became a living person. Then the Lord God planted a garden in Eden in the east, and there He placed the man He had made."

- "The move of God is in your prophetic word to keep you from being stagnant." -Genesis 2:15-17
- "You have the power like a time bomb." -Ecclesiastes 3:1, Ephesians 3:20
- It's your season to reign –"Rejoice and excel through increase and generosity in your now - Mark 10:28-31

You must implement a (NOW) faith purpose concerning your destiny to step into the greater awareness that God has released into your life. It's vital to your development and understanding through kingdom grace that came from God to establish your territory (see Hebrews 11:1-3).

Don't Just Read The Word, You Must Experience It....

That's why God sends His apostles and prophets to decree and declare the word of the Lord through training, activations, teachings, prophetic revelations, impartations, spiritual mentoring and deliverance. The apostolic anointing is a finishing anointing to unlock destiny for success. You must break through barriers and obstacles to overcome generational cycles of peril and destruction. Always spend time around successful people to explode into purpose and destiny for the harvest that comes from God.

A few scriptures to consider; Jesus is a fixer of all things!

Hebrews 5:14 (NASB) – "Solid food is for the mature, who, through training have the skill to recognize the difference between right and wrong."

Hebrews 13:7-8 (NLT) – "Remember your leaders who taught you the Word of God. Think of all the good that has come from their lives, and follow the examples of their faith. Jesus Christ is the same yesterday, today and forever."

We Are Pushing God to Release the Blessings!!!

1. It's your time to be blessed - You need an encore.

2. Time factor of purpose and season - you can be anointed and not appointed for a specific thing.

3. Build your purpose to understand pain through suffering - there must be a time of trial and testing.

4. You must give your problems a letter of divorce - release what is hindering you.

5. Leave the F.R.O.G.S. behind – Foul, Rude, Greedy, and Stink

6. Your pain will produce your purpose -You must have a vision.

7. Pursue your promises because you were born to do something magnificent for God - you are made in the image of Him.

8. Go After It - There is destiny attached to your (IT) Increase and Triumph.

9. Use Everything You Got - Success is your portion, God will silence your enemies.

10. Let your enemies be scattered - don't give the devil a rain check.

11. Praise God for what He is doing now - This is your moment (Embrace Now).

12. Unmerited Favor is in your sights - You got a destiny.

Success will find you at every turn. When you think about how far you have come and the turbulence that you endured, you start to say, "I have a feeling that everything is going to be alright" and there is a peace that comes to your spirit to build your faith.

Six Truths of Communication with God:

1. Your anointing is critical to your future: The power of the anointing is a devotion that rests heavily in our spirit.

2. Communion is your connection to the power of God: Taking daily communion is an act of devotion to remember the sacrifice of our Lord Jesus Christ.

3. Listening is paramount to your spiritual focus and destiny: Purge your ears, mental discipline for your discernment, refresh your mind, body and soul to move your faith in confidence.

4. Speaking brings forth the voice of the spirit of God: Posture your faith by speaking the word of revelation.

5. Fasting and prayer are for spiritual detoxification: Fasting and praying help to redirect your focus and expand your communication levels for more fervent insight with the Lord.

6. Prayer is your foundation: The power of individual prayer, meditation and worship are needed for efficient growth. Your time of communication in prayer unlock success and destiny from the secret holy places in heaven. God is awaiting the arrival of the sons of God to be revealed.

Never limit the ability of God to grant you success and to obtain your destiny. Present yourself before the Father worthy of heavenly treasures. He desires to blow your mind. Will you allow Him to show up and show out like only He can on your behalf? Be ready for success and be ready to embrace your destiny. There is a place you must get to for the glory of God. Therefore, praise Him in advance because your blessings are quickly moving in your direction.

Success + Destiny = God-ordained miracles, signs and wonders.

Hebrews 2:4 (ESV) – "While God also bore witness, by signs and wonders and various miracles, and by gifts of the Holy Spirit, distributed according to His will."

CHAPER 9

THE WALK IS WORTH IT...

Walking is a great form of exercise and cardio. It gives you the opportunity for clear thinking and relief from any stressors that may be preventing you from sound decisions. Continue to walk with confidence, love, maturity and grace. In doing so, you will receive the revelation that the walk is worth it.

Walk -

1. Move at a regular pace by lifting and setting down each foot in turn, never having both feet off of the ground at once.
2. Guide, accompany, or escort (someone) on foot.
3. Abandon or suddenly withdraw from a job, commitment, or situation.

Walk -

A. An act of traveling or an excursion on foot.
B. A route recommended or marked out for recreational walking.
C. An unhurried rate of movement on foot.
D. A part of a forest under one keeper.

Just a thought:

Your spiritual life is not compared by how much you talk about the Lord, but how closely your walk is with the Lord.

Colossians 1:10 (NASB) – "Walk in a manner worthy of the Lord, to please Him in all respects, bearing fruit in every good work and increasing in the knowledge of God."

Deuteronomy 5:33 (KJV) – "Ye shall walk in all the ways which the Lord your God hath commanded you, that ye may live, and [that it may be] well with you, and [that] ye may prolong [your] days in the land which ye shall possess."

Ephesians 2:10 (KJV) – "For we are His workmanship, created in Christ Jesus unto good works, which God hath before ordained that we should walk in them."

2 Corinthians 5:7(KJV) – "For we walk by faith, not by sight."

Faith is something that is difficult to process mentally during different stages of your journey. Faith is about an abiding belief in your humanity and spirituality. Therefore, you must keep a humble heart throughout the peaks and valleys of life. The Bible declares in James 4:6 (NASB) – "God is opposed to the proud but gives grace to the humble."

Having humility and faith will coincide for a victory during circumstances. Faith is about your belief in the future and beyond limits of your current conditions. Remember this, "faith is not

DR. FREDRICK J. HARRIS

a religion"; it is derived from your relationship with God. The abiding belief is in the visions, dreams, plans and revelations He has given you. When you've made a decision to walk by faith and know that this process is worth it, wisdom and knowledge can lead you into a place of faith, power, and dominion like never before.

"Faith is the substance of things hoped for and the evidence of things not seen." (see Hebrews 11:1)

As the walk of your life is unfolding before you, there will be encounters you'll have with God along the way. I would like to reveal three encounters that will bring insight for further understanding:

Prophetic Encounters with God:

1. Invitation - you must invite God into your situation and allow Him to take control for the solution.

2. Impartation - receive the direction that the Father in heaven shall reveal to you in your communication with Him.

3. Revelation - open visions shall be explored as the Lord takes you into higher

dimensions with power through His presence. This will give strength to see it according to the plan of God.

Here are things to consider while walking through this process:

- Everybody and everything from your past are not a part of your future.
- You have reason and purpose on your side, which is the Holy Spirit.
- Make sure your motives are in alignment with God and His direction.
- Do self-assessments to stay on task with your vision.

Proverbs 16:2 (GNT) – "You may think everything you do is right, but the Lord judges your motives."

Many people have conversations frequently about having faith and trusting God through it all. You must exercise the gift that the Lord has given you. I implore you to speak with the authority that's in your mouth, speaking those things that are not as they are.

The life that God wants to give of Himself to us is far better than the life you will anticipate building for yourself.

John 10:10 (NLT) states, "The thief's purpose is to steal and kill and destroy. My purpose is to give life in all its fullness."

I will start this conversation with this statement:

Be passionate about your purpose. You must walk with a pursuit of determination and be strengthened by the Lord to complete your quest. There must be something innately on the inside of you that must be activated for such a time as now. God has given you power and dominion to go after everything He has reserved in the kingdom for you and your life. Now is the time to act and to get motivated for these ambitions to live. Your blessings have your name on them, which means you have an assignment and directive by God to go for it.

Do you have an inner peace about your walk? Are you ready for overflow and increase? Do you have what it takes to step out in faith?

I ask these questions as a prerequisite, because there are many conversations about "I'm going to start my dreams now", but then years later you're still in the same place. Why is that? Because excuses are easy, but trust is submission. We have inclined our ear to hear the Lord, sowing seeds of various capacities to positively impact lives of those who love God.

As you build your networks, connections and relationships, it is very important to remember that those seeds will grow when they are sown the right way through love, humility, and grace. God desires to truly honor our obedience and willingness to believe, not giving up. Do it according to His will, and you will not regret this decision.

2 Corinthians 8:14 - "At this present time, your plenty will supply what they need, so that, in turn, their plenty will supply what you need. There will be equality."

1 Timothy 5:17(NIV) – "The elders who direct the affairs of the church well are worthy of double honor, especially those whose work is preaching and teaching."

Luke 4:18-19 (NIV) - "The Spirit of the Lord is on me, because he has anointed me to preach the good news to the poor. He has sent me to proclaim freedom for the prisoners and recovery of sight for the blind, to release the oppressed, to proclaim the year of the Lord's favor."

- Favor equals Anointed to Impact or Influenced which returns the love of Christ Jesus!

Throughout these chapters, my hope is that you Embrace Your Moment....

Be inspired to grab your vision and prepare a legacy that cannot be erased.

Hard work is the bridge to diligence in all things necessary for blessings. Look at how far you have traveled in your life. You must see yourself as valuable; don't neglect the capabilities inside of you. I listen to people from all different walks of life say, "this walk is lonely". My answer to that statement is "who told you that you were alone"?

But what would make a person take on this way of thinking about doing things alone? There is an array of questions that go unanswered. I believe it comes from a way of thinking that was introduced to a person's life.

For generations there have been so much information given to us, but much of what we have gathered from the previous generation has not been taught to us. It was merely passed down from one generation to the next. Because of this, many of us assumed we were doing the right thing, not realizing it caused us to veer off course from the plan orchestrated by God. Therefore, mistakes and errors become synonymous to our understanding, so we take on a mind of failure and not progress.

The information and technology age are at an all-time high. Everything that you need is right at the click of a mouse on your computer, or a swipe on your phone. It's so amazing how convenient most things are available to consumers. Believe it or not, we are a nation, and people, of consumption in just about everything. The hope is for you to have the same tenacious approach about your walk of success in the knowledge of God as you are with the cares of society.

Nobody who has achieved a great level of success and prosperity in their life and chosen professions, didn't experience extraordinary setbacks. Nothing is handed to you for the most part; unless you were born with a lot of wealth and people doing everything for you. Those individuals are amongst us as well. Just observe their demeanor towards life and others. You will see a disposition of attitude and entitlement, also a strong, prideful spirit. They are disconnected from the reality of people who have everyday challenges.

I grew up in the south and lived in underprivileged housing apartments. My parents never had much from a material standpoint, but they did the best they could with what they had. As I got older and started to mature, I knew what it meant to work hard and be a man of integrity. I began to seek out the older generation for answers and understandings, because I wanted more than what I could see and experience while growing up. Many of them would say to me, "Don't end up like us. Go and do something good with your life."

It was sad to hear this, but refreshing to know that I had a chance to make a difference for something great. I remained very positive and focused to know that every adversity was an opportunity for greatness. This is difficult to embrace, but this walk is worth it.

Your Kingdom Assignment Is Greater Than Any Distraction:

1. No More Excuses - if you are going to be great, then you must eradicate every excuse.

2. Establish Healthy Relationships - who you are with and where you spend your time are crucial ingredients during this walk.

3. Eat the Fruit of Success not Serpents - what you digest can make you sluggish and sleepy or make you stable and sound.

4. Manage your Money - monitor where you spend and always guard your investments.

5. Continue your Education - galvanize wisdom, both spiritually and naturally. Have a love of learning.

Walk into Promises by Faith:

I charge you, as you are reading this book, to hold onto the promises of faith in God. Our ancestors did the best they could and only reached a level of success that they could understand. You have the chance to be great and it does not mean you have to become a millionaire to do so. I believe that it is fundamentally wrong to deceive people, saying everyone is going to be rich. This is a false narrative that a lot of Americans and believers in Christ have fallen to this spirit of manipulation. If people are equipped the right way through teaching and training, our society will be in such a better place of love and harmony. However, many have this illusion of wealth and prosperity and fail to acknowledge that God desires for us to be in good health so that our soul shall prosper (see 3 John 2).

E M B R A C E   Y O U R   M O M E N T

This walk is worth it if we:

A. Maintain our standards and do not compromise

B. Set realistic goals and trust the process.

C. Listen to advisors and mentors that you respect and value.

D. Have confidence that the outlook is going to be great.

E. Attend workshops, conferences and seminars to enhance your education.

F. Research certification programs to help build your financial portfolio.

G. Challenge yourself by spending time in meditation.

H. Release all frustration and agitation from past failures.

I. Don't lose your zeal as you are moving progressively.

CHAPTER 10

THE BEST IS STILL TO COME
(I'm Not Done Yet)

In this final chapter of the book, we have made mention of several topics and wisdom keys that I pray have given you greater insight. You must know and appreciate that the best is still to come. You have more in front of you than what is left behind. Focus your sights and adjust your compass for everything that is waiting at the finish line of your faith.

Marathon: a long-lasting or difficult task or operation of a specified kind

1. A long-distance running race, strictly one of twenty-six miles
2. A footrace run on an open course usually of twenty-six miles, 385 yards
3. An endurance contest
4. An event or activity that requires prolonged effort, endurance or attention.

Scripture: Ecclesiastes 9:11(KJV) – "I returned, and saw under the sun, that the race is not to the swift, nor the battle to the strong, neither yet bread to the wise, nor yet riches to men of understanding, nor yet favor to men of skill; but time and chance happeneth to them all."

Race: Verb
Compete with another, or others, to see who is fastest at covering a set course or achieving an objective.

Move or progress swiftly or at full speed.

Noun

1. A competition between runners, horses, vehicles, boats, etc., to see which is the fastest in covering a set course.

2. A strong or rapid current flowing through a narrow channel in the sea or a river.

3. A water channel, especially one built to lead water to or from a point where its energy is utilized, as in a mill or mine. (Millrace)

4. A smooth ring-shaped groove or guide, in which a ball bearing or roller bearing runs.

   - Race refers to a person's physical characteristics; such as, .bone structure and skin, hair, or eye color.
   - Ethnicity refers to cultural factors, including nationality and sociological factors, respectively.
   - Regional culture, ancestry, and language are components of a race as well.

Throughout our lives, we have overcome many challenges in very sensitive areas. From social to economic diversities, there are broad discussions across the political spectrum, the spiritual climate in churches, social advocacy in communities and schools, and the way our nation is governed today. All this comes back to race; not the sense of color of skin or ethnic background, but one that has to do with your journey.

- How are you defined by your race?
- What are the driving forces behind your race?
- What have you learned during your marathon?
- And where do you go from here?

These are amazing questions to ask yourself, because everybody wants to win their race. My point is, have you gone before God and asked Him to show you the course of your race or marathon?

Life is grueling, audacious, laboring and overwhelming at times. Then you flip to the other side and life is good, blessed, loving, considerate, rewarding, happy, fruitful and replenishing.

In this chapter I want you who are reading this to know: The Best is Still to Come...

You are just like an Olympic athlete! You train hard for months, or even years. Now here you are, in the starting blocks of the race, and you know it's so important to get off the block with a good start, whether it's track and field or swimming, you already set your sights on how this race is going to end with you standing on top of the podium while the whole world watches.

You still have a way to go and it's not time to quit or throw in the towel. Here are a few scriptures and people in the Bible to consider concerning your race:

1. Abraham - Genesis 12:1-3 (ESV) – "Now the Lord said to Abram, "Go from your country and your kindred and your father's house to the land that I will show you. And I will make you a great nation, and I will bless you and make your name great, so that you be a blessing. I will bless those who bless you, and him who dishonors you I

will curse, and in you all the families of the earth shall be blessed."

2. Moses - Exodus 3:2-12 (TLB) – "Suddenly, the Angel of Jehovah appeared to him as a flame of fire in a bush. When Moses saw that the bush was on fire and that it didn't burn up, he went over to investigate. Then God called out to him, "Moses! Moses!" "Who is it?" Moses asked. "Don't come any closer," God told him. "Take off your shoes, for you are standing on holy ground. I am the God of your fathers - the God of Abraham, Isaac, and Jacob." (Moses covered his face with his hands, for he was afraid to look at God.) Then the Lord told him, "I have seen the deep sorrows of my people in Egypt and have heard their pleas for freedom from their harsh taskmasters. I have come to deliver them from the Egyptians and to take them out of Egypt into a good land, a large land, a land flowing with milk and honey- the land where the Canaanites,

Hittites, Amorites, Perizzites, Hivites, and Jebusites live. Yes, the wail of the people of Israel has risen to me in heaven, and I have seen the heavy tasks the Egyptians have oppressed them with. Now I am going to send you to Pharaoh, to demand that he let you lead my people out of Egypt." "But I'm not the person for a job like that!" Moses exclaimed. Then God told him, "I will certainly be with you, and this is the proof that I am the one who is sending you: When you have led the people out of Egypt, you shall worship God here upon this mountain!"

3. Joseph - Genesis 39:2 (TLB) – "The Lord greatly blessed Joseph there in the home of his master, so that everything he did succeeded."

4. David - 1 Samuel 30:8 (AMP) – "David inquired of the Lord, saying, "Shall I pursue this band [of raiders]? Will I overtake

them?" And He answered him, "Pursue, for you will certainly overtake them, and you will certainly rescue [the captives]."

5. Jesus - Luke 2:51-52 (NCV) – "Jesus went with them to Nazareth and was obedient to them. But His mother kept in her mind all that had happened. Jesus became wiser and grew physically. People liked Him, and He pleased God.

6. Paul - Acts 23:11 (NLT) – "That night the Lord appeared to Paul and said, "Be encouraged, Paul. Just as you have been a witness to me here in Jerusalem, you must preach the Good News in Rome as well."

Now, can you see how God used all of these people (to include Jesus) for His glory? He will do the same with you also. I just want to encourage you that your race is not done yet; the best is still yet to come.

Think of all of the things that you have not accomplished yet and put a demand on your faith, that you will start from where you are and go forward. Not rehashing things from your past that caused so much detriment; it prevented you from totally seeing it through the eyes of the Lord. The previous generations could not get it done. Many of them did not know and there was also a great level of distress that accompanied the way they would think, and respond, to problems of becoming established and how to solve them.

> "Whereby, when ye read, ye can perceive my understanding in the mystery of Christ; which in other generations was not made known unto the sons of men, as it hath now been revealed unto His holy apostles and prophets in the Spirit."
>
> -Ephesians 3:4-5 (ASV)

CONCLUSION

There is a mandate for you to accomplish your plans. I encourage you to dream big. Your story is so great that it takes a lifetime to tell it. "God can bless you exceedingly and abundantly above all you could ask or think." (Ephesians 3:20)

Believe in God and believe in your abilities to run your race with grace, wisdom, faith, power and maturity. You will get there and win the prize, but it must be done with God as the center piece. Always look through your periscope; travel the seas of your understanding and watch God truly take care of you.

You are a champion; you are on your way to greatness. You have tremendous miracles ahead of you. Your journey is only beginning, because the Best is Still to Come!

You're Not Done Yet...
EMBRACE YOUR MOMENT
(Building a Legacy that Can't Be Erased)
Blessings in Jesus name,

Micah 6:8
1 Corinthians 14:33
2 Corinthians 5:18

ABOUT THE AUTHOR

Dr. Fredrick J. Harris is a licensed and ordained Minister, Pastor, Prophet, and Apostle. He walks humbly for God in the Apostolic and Prophetic anointing, and the continuous work in the ministry of God. Born in Sumter, South Carolina, on February 4, 1972, Dr. Harris enlisted in the United States Army shortly after high school and college; he served with distinction and honor, and retired with 26 years of impeccable service to the Nation, and is a War Hero and Decorated Veteran. Apostle Harris joined the United States Army in 2000, and continues to be the leader God ordained him to be before the foundation of the earth. He has extensive military training, which has allowed him the opportunity to touch an abundant amount of soldiers' lives. His life has touched many in his military tenure and still does. He is a leading example of Christ on earth as he teaches the soldiers to follow him as he follows Christ.

Apostle Harris has participated in Ministry Teams on two tours to Iraq 2003 and 2005, and one tour to Afghanistan 2012; glory to God. He has been teaching Bible Studies since 2006 in three locations: Oklahoma, South Carolina, and North Carolina. In November 2009, he was ordained as a Minister at Greenlawn Baptist Church in Columbia, South Carolina. He was a part of an International Bible Study Teaching from France 2010-2011. In October 2011, he was ordained into Prophetic Ministry at Zoe Ministries in New York, NY. In January 2012, he was ordained as an Apostle/Prophet/Pastor in Greenville, South Carolina. On May 5, 2012, he was ordained Apostolic Leader and Founder of Without Limits Fellowship Ministries in Raeford, North Carolina. Apostle Harris was later reaffirmed and consecrated to the Office of the Apostle at Faith and Power Christian Center in Dunn, North Carolina.

Apostle Harris is an Apostle of Reconciliation and Peace with a passion to impact the world through the Gospel of Jesus Christ. He has travelled to Germany, Kuwait, Ireland, Iraq, Afghanistan, Kyrgyzstan, Belgium, and the Bahamas through military and ministerial opportunities to teach and preach the Gospel of Jesus Christ. He has acquired substantial wisdom through life experiences and education. He is the founder of Without Limits Fellowship Ministries, Heart of God Embassy, Land of Goshen Christian Center, and the WLMI Ministry School and Training Academy, which is located in Raleigh, North Carolina, and two Bible Study Ministries, the City of Jerusalem Worship Center and Feet in the Breeze Military Ministry Bible Study, with an extended teaching venue to minister at Womack Army Hospital on Fort Bragg, North Carolina.

He is also the Senior Instructor at WLMI School of Apostolic and Prophetic Ministry. He has evangelized, ministered, counseled, and taught the Gospel of Jesus Christ to well over 35,000 soldiers and civilians in various capacities worldwide.

Education and learning are extremely important to Apostle Harris, as a devout leader in the Body of Christ. He has received his Doctoral degree in Philosophy and Christian Education, and a Master of Divinity from Omni Bible University International.

He has received a certification in Military Science and Health Management from North Central Institute in Clarksville, Tennessee, and he is also certified in Spiritual Empowerment and Resiliency at the University of Pennsylvania in Philadelphia, PA. He was also honored by the University of Michigan as a Survey Team Coordinator for successful implementation of the Army STARRS (Study to Assess Risk and Resilience in Service Members) Program, conducting studies for ongoing health promotion, risk reduction, and suicide prevention efforts.

He is currently pursuing educational opportunities in Network Communications Management.

Dr. Harris is also a Certified Christian Life Coach Professional through Freedom Bible College in Wilmington, Delaware. His role is to assist individuals and clients to achieve success in their personal and professional lives, in keeping with moral and scriptural foundational truths. Dr. Fredrick J. Harris is the host of Apostle's Corner Live Stream Broadcast in Fayetteville, North Carolina, and the Freedom & Fire TV/Radio Broadcast in Clinton, North Carolina.

These are monthly broadcasts that can be heard worldwide on the airwaves, local cable television, plus the internet through social media platforms of Facebook (Live) and Periscope. Apostle's radio talk show is an extension of the WLM Outreach Ministry, impacting and encouraging the community, the nation, and the world into a closer relationship with the Lord Jesus Christ.

Dr. Fredrick J. Harris is a prophetic scribe who has authored several books and a stage play. He is the author of "Keep Moving Forward", "Footprints of a King", "The Boomerang Effect", and "God's Grace and A Soldier's Love", (the book and stage play).

These anointed resources have given birth to "Kingdom Keys and "M.A.N.N.A, Miraculous Appearance of Necessary Nourishment from The Almighty/Acronyms for Kingdom Building" (now retired and no longer in print). He is also a contribution writer for 'Military News with Oasis Montage' Magazine. All of these anointed aspirations have been birthed out of the heart of God, for the people of God.

He currently resides near Raleigh, North Carolina with his wife (Lady) LaKendra, and their sons Marquez, Christian, and Marley.

www.ingramcontent.com/pod-product-compliance
Lightning Source LLC
Chambersburg PA
CBHW071805090426
42737CB00012B/1953